GOLDEN GOD

Jeanne DuPrau

LEARNING · DEVELOPMENT · AIDS

LDA

Golden God
LD875R
ISBN 1 85503 016 0

Published under licence in the UK by LDA

First published in UK 1990

LDA, Duke Street, Wisbech, Cambs., PE13 2AE England

Printed in Great Britain by Ebenezer Baylis and Son Ltd,
The Trinity Press, Worcester, and London.

CHAPTER

1

The Discovery

The stone that suddenly appeared was about a foot long and several inches thick. It was flat and smooth. Quickly the Arab worker put down his shovel and began to dig around it with his fingers. As he uncovered more and more of the long, flat stone, he felt sure it was no ordinary one. Human hands had shaped this one – probably thousands of years ago.

"Dr. Selk! Dr. Selk!" the worker shouted as he started climbing up the ladder out of the pit. "Dr. Selk!"

A short man in jeans and a worn shirt came running across the sand. As he passed the mess tent, a young woman in old khaki trousers, bright T-shirt, and sun hat looked up. "Have they found something?" she called to the man hurrying past her.

For an answer, the man waved to the woman to follow. And he continued on his way toward the pit at the far end of the camp.

Val Randolph pushed her hat on more tightly and started to follow the running figure across the burning white sand. For a moment, the hot afternoon sun made her feel light-headed. But she felt better quickly and ran to catch up with Selk.

By the time Val got to him, Selk had reached the side of the pit. He was looking down into the deep hole and breathing quickly. Val looked down too. A square, flat stone rested at the bottom.

This is it, Val thought. This is what we've been looking for all these months. Dr. Selk was an archaeologist and Val was his assistant. They were looking for an old city that had been buried.

In a moment, she was following Selk down the ladder into the pit. The workers had gathered near the deep hole, and Val could hear their excited voices as she lowered herself into it. Then, as soon as she reached the bottom, she dropped to her knees next to Selk.

He was running his hands lightly over the stone. Finally he nodded, sat back, and smiled. "Well," he said. "Well, I think we've found something at last." Still smiling, he called up to the workers in words of Arabic to let them know what had happened below.

Selk's voice was calm. But Val had known the archaeologist long enough to tell that he was excited. He had never been one to show his feelings. But Val had taken classes from him at the University of California and been his assistant for a year on this dig. She could sense the way he held himself back.

"Let's get started," Selk said to her now. Then he added, "Where is Bruce?"

"Lying down, I think," Val answered.

Selk just shook his head. Then together he and Val began to dig away the dirt that remained around the bottom of the stone. They forced themselves to work carefully and slowly. And it paid off. Soon they saw another square stone beneath the first one. Then another. It looked as if the blocks formed a wall.

They dug on without speaking. But Val's mind was spinning. She remembered the first time Selk had spoken to her about this part of the desert. It had been after a class, and she had been fascinated. "The city should be somewhere in this area," Selk had said. His thin finger pointed to an empty space on the map. He had smiled as he spoke, his voice warm and alive.

Selk believed that an ancient city had once stood where they were now digging. His early life in the area and later his studies had made him think this corner of the desert held valuable pieces of history. He had long hoped to find them.

Selk was given his chance. The university gave him a grant to head an archaeological dig in his home country of Kalim for two summers. The first summer, he had asked Val, a top student, to be his assistant. They had worked hard, but nothing had been found. This second summer, Selk had taken another student assistant, Bruce Carver, along with him and Val. And he had moved the dig to a place a short distance away. There they had worked two long hot months and found nothing until today.

When the sun went down, a door in a long wall had been uncovered. But the doorway was filled with more blocks of stone that would take hours to remove. That work would have to wait until the next day. The excitement in the camp grew, and sleep was slow in coming.

At dawn, a dim light made its way into the ring of small tents around the camp. Val woke up to it, dressed quickly, and went outside. She looked around. Coloured cracks were beginning to spread through the sky. The deep pits where work had gone on all summer and the hills of dirt and rock next to them looked strange in the early morning light.

It wasn't yet hot. Walking quickly, Val headed to the pit where the wall had been uncovered and looked down. At the bottom, next to the stone wall, she saw a light.

"Dr. Selk!" she called.

He turned and waved up at her. "You're up early," he said.

"Did you really expect me to sleep late?" said Val. "Today?"

Selk smiled and turned back to his work. Val was about to climb down the ladder and join him when she heard a voice behind her.

"So this is the famous wall," the voice said. "Will an 'Open, Sesame!' help get the stones out?"

Val turned around laughing. "No," she said. "But another pair of hands will. Let's get going."

Bruce Carver, the other student assistant, followed Val down the ladder. "In a way I'm glad those stones are there," he said. "I missed all the excitement yesterday when the first one was found. The heat of the morning really did me in. I felt so sick I had to lie down. I can't believe I slept through the first find of the dig. But at least I can help today."

Selk only nodded at Bruce as the young man started to work next to him. Bruce, like Val, was a very good student. But unlike Val, Bruce had had trouble in the field from the first day. No matter how he protected himself, the hot desert sun burned his skin again and again. It often made him feel sick, and he would have to stop working. Though he loved archaeology and had enjoyed other digs, this one had not been easy for him.

But this morning, in the cool early hours, Bruce was cheerful. He worked with great energy. By nine he and Val and Selk had taken enough stones from the doorway to make a two-foot hole.

Holding his torch, Selk put his arm through the hole, and then his head. Val and Bruce waited for his report. "What do you see?" Val asked finally.

"It's hard to tell," Selk answered slowly. "It's a room, I think. Or maybe a tunnel. There's a stone roof."

They went back to work. As the heat of the day grew, Bruce slowed down, but Val found herself working faster and faster. Finally Selk had to ask her to slow down. "Whatever is in there won't go away," he said. "We have to be just as careful now as we always have been. These rocks probably haven't been touched for thousands of years, remember. If we do the wrong thing, we could bring them all down on our heads."

Bruce gave a nervous laugh at that, but Val saw the way he looked at the rocks. It seemed as if his cheerful manner was quickly disappearing.

It was just noon when they pulled the last rock from the doorway and turned their torches into the opening. And there in front of them was a tunnel about 2 metres high. It led straight back from the doorway, and it seemed to get smaller as it reached into the distance. "Let's take a look inside," Selk said quietly.

With his torch showing the way, Selk stepped into the tunnel. Val and Bruce followed. There was a chill in the tunnel air, in spite of the heat outside. The walls were dark and still. It seemed to the three archaeologists that suddenly they were very far from the world they knew.

They wondered where the tunnel would take them. But they didn't have far to go to find out. About 15 metres in the tunnel ended at another door. And it was blocked with stones just like the first one.

Bruce groaned, but Val turned quickly back to get their tools and lamps in the outer room. Selk's face showed nothing at all as he began to work again, digging around the heavy stones in the doorway.

The going was even slower this time. Since they were now far under the sand, no sunlight reached them. Lamps and torches alone had to light their work. And these threw shadows that made it hard to see what they were doing.

The three also soon discovered that the stones were crammed very tightly into the doorway. After an hour, they were still working on the first stone at the top of the doorway. Val was beginning to think the big rock would never move. Then, all at once, it did.

They had been cutting on both sides of the stone, and every few minutes, Selk had tested to see if it would come loose. This time as he pulled, the stone came out about 12 cms. "That's a start," he said. "Let's keep at it."

But before they could begin again, they heard a sudden frightening noise – a cracking, grinding noise. The stones in the roof above the doorway began to fall. Streams of dirt poured down. A stone the size of a big orange hit Bruce on his hand, knocking away his chipping tool.

"Run!" Selk yelled in a voice Val had never heard him use before. "Back through the tunnel to the outside! Quick!"

Holding their arms over their heads, the three ran out of the tunnel and into the pit. They climbed the ladder and then stood, listening and watching.

The cave-in didn't last long. When the sounds stopped and the dust settled, Selk picked up his light and turned it on. "Time to see what it looks like inside," he said.

Bruce looked at Selk in surprise. "You're going back in there?" he asked, rubbing some dirt from his face.

"Of course," Selk said. "We all are." He peered at Bruce for a moment, but it was hard to tell what he was thinking. "I need everyone's help on this," he said at last. "We'll dig out what's fallen, then make the rest safe. There's no need to worry."

Bruce didn't look very pleased with Selk's words. Val could see that his hand shook as he picked up his torch. Then Selk spoke again. "Bruce, why don't you find Ali before coming back to work here? Help him bring over some of the heavy beams piled up in the main camp. We can use them to hold up the tunnel roof and protect ourselves from further cave-ins."

Bruce looked happy at the thought of putting off his next trip into the tunnel. With a fast nod, he hurried off to find Ali, the head of the Arab workers at the dig.

Val watched Bruce leave. Then she picked up a shovel and turned on her torch. She climbed down the ladder and stepped into the rock-filled tunnel. Then slowly she walked to the far end where Selk was already working.

It took over an hour to clear away the rocks and dirt. As Val and Selk worked, Bruce and Ali brought beam after beam down the ladder and to the doorway. Ali, in his white robe and red-checked headpiece, worked quickly and quietly. He said nothing about the cave-in or the blocked doorway as he carried the heavy wood.

Bruce, too, worked quietly. Once he had stepped into the tunnel again, he became less worried about a second cave-in. But he seemed even happier when he helped Selk and Val place the beams against the walls and ceiling.

With the beams in place, Selk pulled the first stone all the way out of the doorway. The ceiling held. Breathing deeply, they then began working on the stone next to the first one. Soon it too came out. Now there was a hole in the doorway big enough to look through.

"Val, hand me that strong lamp," said Selk. She passed it to him, and he put it through the hole and looked in. For a long moment, he was silent. Val and Bruce waited for him to say something, hardly breathing. "What do you see?" Bruce finally asked, running his fingers quickly through his hair.

Instead of answering, Selk stepped away from the hole. "Look for yourselves," he said, handing the lamp first to Val. His voice was low and quiet. His face showed nothing.

Val moved the lamp into the darkness behind the wall. Then she looked through the hole into a small, square room. At first she saw only stones – more stone walls, another stone ceiling. Then, as she pointed the lamp at one corner, the light came to rest on something large and bright. Val caught her breath. "A golden statue!" she whispered. She had never seen anything like it. It was almost a metre tall and looked like solid gold.

CHAPTER

2

Through the Doorway

It took almost three hours to get the rest of the stones out of the doorway. In the desert beyond the tunnel, the sun set and darkness came. But none of the three archaeologists cared. Their look at the golden figure had made them forget that they were tired and hungry.

At last the doorway was open. Selk, Val, and Bruce stepped through it and into the room beyond. They beamed their lights into the corner as they walked slowly toward the statue. It seemed to look back at them as if it was alive. Val and Selk reached out and touched its golden head and green stone eyes. But Bruce only stared, unable to move his hand forward. The statue wasn't beautiful or ugly, but the half-smile and knowing look on its face gave it an other-world feeling.

Selk bent down to look at the short, fat figure more closely. He played his light over some odd markings on its back and stomach. They were short, rounded lines, almost like writing. He shook his head, lost in thought.

"Dr. Selk," said Bruce at last, pulling his eyes away from the statue's strange face. "What is this?"

Selk sat back on his heels. "Well," he answered, his voice still quiet. "It might be easier to say what it *isn't*. It isn't like the art of any other ancient people from this part of the world. It isn't from the time period that I had expected – it seems to be from an older one. I would guess that it's the figure of a god. But what god, I don't know. It will take some time to place it."

For a few more minutes, Selk continued to look at the golden god, peering at it from every side. Then he said, "We'll leave it where it is now and come back tomorrow." With a small smile, he told Val and Bruce they had done a good day's work. Then, hurrying up the ladder and outside, he called for an Arab worker to guard the tunnel during the night.

As Val and Bruce reached the top of the ladder, they could see Selk heading quickly for his tent.

The two assistants moved towards their own tents more slowly. The light of several pit fires threw shadows across the white sands where they walked.

"Weird-looking, isn't it?" Bruce asked.

"Yes," Val agreed, nodding her tired head. But her voice was full of excitement. "It looks like it knows some terrible secret it isn't about to tell."

Bruce made a noise like a laugh. "You know the curses that were put on those tombs in Egypt," he said. "According to stories, awful things happened to people who went into the tombs. Maybe there's a curse like that on the tomb of this golden god."

"And what's the secret it knows?" asked Val, smiling. "That we're all going to come down with some terrible sickness or something?"

"Why not?" Bruce reached out and stopped Val. "Did you see its eyes? And that smile? It certainly looks weird enough to be cursed."

Val crossed her arms. "That statue will put no curse on us," she said strongly. "It's an important find, I bet." Then she smiled again. "Who knows? Maybe it will make us all famous. There's no way it could bring us bad luck."

* * *

The next day, work on bringing the statue out of its rock-lined room began. Bruce took pictures of the god with his camera and recorded its size and markings. Then several Arab workers brought a small wagon and some blankets and rope down the tunnel. The statue was wrapped first. Then it was lifted carefully onto the wagon and tied down for its trip to the outside. Strong hands and more ropes were waiting to pull the heavy statue to the top of the pit.

Everyone gathered to peer at the strange golden god again in the light of day. The Arabs all around pointed excitedly at the green eyes and knowing face. But Selk had the statue quickly brought to his tent to be safely stored. Then he returned with Val and Bruce to begin digging again in the tunnel and small room. Other things might still be buried – things that would tell something about the statue's history.

One handful at a time, they hunted through the sand. They dug into the walls and ceiling and poked into all the cracks between the stones. They worked their way deeper into the floor with small picks. And they sifted every bit of sand.

"There ought to be more artifacts here," Selk kept saying when nothing was found. "Rings, jars, pieces of pots . . . anything. This is very strange."

The rest of the week was spent looking in the dirt, but still nothing was uncovered. Finally Selk decided to look in a new place – just west of the spot where they had made their find. A new hole was dug, and the search went on.

One afternoon Val and Selk were working alone. Bruce had gone back to his tent to lie down, feeling ill. Val was on her hands and knees, pawing through the sand in a corner of the pit. Selk was a short distance away, his back to her.

The sun beat down on them as they worked. It was the hottest part of the day. Val's shirt stuck to her back, and the dust made her cough. She sat back after a while to wipe the sweat from her face. As she did, she looked over toward Selk. He was bending forward to look closely at something on the ground. While she watched, Selk reached out and picked up a handful of sand.

He's found something! Val thought. She was just about to ask him what it was when he did something that surprised her. Selk took a small clear bag from his pocket – the kind that finds were kept in – and put the sand into it. Then, saying nothing, he put the bag into his pocket and went on working.

Val sat without moving. How strange, she thought. I wonder why he didn't say anything to me. Selk had always been free with his ideas and discoveries. It was unthinkable that he would keep something important to himself. But it seemed as though he just had.

Val turned back to her work, pulling the top of her shirt away from her wet neck. Maybe it was just an interesting stone, she thought as she dug into the sand again. Or maybe he wants to keep going now and will show me what he found later. She had to believe that he would.

At last the sun began to dip low in the sky, and the air grew cooler. Selk stood up. "That's enough for today," he said, his face calm. "We'll look again tomorrow."

Now, thought Val. He'll tell me what's in the bag. But Selk said nothing. Instead he followed Val up the ladder and turned toward the mess tent.

"Isn't it strange we haven't found anything else?" Val called after him. "I didn't turn up a single thing today."

Selk stopped and looked back. "Neither did I," he said.

Val's heart sank. "Nothing at all?" she asked.

Selk stared at her, a strange look on his face. "No," he said. "Not a thing."

CHAPTER

3

The Visitor

Val walked slowly after Selk. Stars were beginning to shine in the deep blue-green sky. The lights from the mess tent burned warmly, and the smell of dinner floated lightly in the air. But Val noticed none of it. Doubts and questions filled her mind. All she wanted to do was sit quietly and think.

"I don't feel very well," she told Selk when she found him in the mess tent. "I think I'll skip dinner tonight."

Selk looked surprised. "First Bruce and now you," he said, "Is the work getting to you?"

Val tried to smile. "I'm just tired," she said.

When she got to her tent, Val lay down without even lighting the oil lamp. She stared into the dark, trying to think. I won't tell anyone what happened, she thought to herself. Before I do, I'll wait to see if there's a reason for his hiding his find. But what reason could there be?

Tired from work and worry, Val closed her eyes. Sounds from outside her tent floated in to her – Arab workers talking, the call of night birds. Then came Selk's voice, clear and calm, as he spoke with Ali. Val's spinning thoughts slowed down. Her stiff body grew more quiet. She began to fall asleep.

Suddenly a shout brought her awake with a start. More shouts followed, and there was the sound of running feet. Val jumped up and ran out of her tent. Ali, his red and white headpiece flying out behind him, was running by. "What is it?" Val called to him.

"Someone is arriving," Ali called back. And then Val saw for herself. A jeep with large tyres and carrying two passengers was pulling into the centre of the camp. When it stopped, a man in a long, white robe, jumped out of the back. Selk walked to him. It looked to Val as if the two men met warmly. But she was too far away to hear what they were saying. She began to walk toward them.

Ahead of her, Bruce was walking towards Selk and the man too. Val walked faster, and she quickly caught up with Bruce. "Who do you think that is?" she asked, nodding at the man who was talking with Selk. As they looked over, they saw him moving his arms and pointing around.

"I don't know," Bruce answered. "He seems to be a friend of Dr. Selk's. He doesn't look too happy though." Bruce was close enough now to see the dark look on the man's face.

"Bruce, Val." Selk had seen the two of them walking up and was waving them over. "This is my friend Machmoud," he said when they were closer. Machmoud bowed low to Val and Bruce, and they smiled back at the short, thin man with deep-set eyes.

"I'm afraid Machmoud has brought bad news," Selk went on. "The government of Kalim has been taken over – by force. The capital is in the hands of rebels now."

"Many members of the old government have already been shot," Machmoud went on. "The rebels have set up their own police force, and though I believe they are no more than simple killers, they are now in power. At this moment, they are out looking for people who were friendly to the old government. They are also jailing people with money and taking their riches. They say they are taking the money 'for the people,' but I am sure they mean for themselves. They are even looking for people who are not from Kalim."

"Like us?" Bruce asked quickly. He crossed his arms tightly. "We're not from Kalim – but we're not making any trouble."

Machmoud looked at Bruce, then at Selk and Val. "The rebels would probably say you *are* making trouble – that you are trying to steal what belongs to the people of Kalim."

"Things the rebels would destroy and sell for the gold anyway, I'll bet," Selk broke in with an angry voice. "If they took the statue, it would never be seen by one person from Kalim. They would destroy it too."

"What about us?" Bruce asked Machmoud. "What would they do if they thought we were trouble for them?"

Machmoud shrugged. "Who knows? But I would have to believe you are no longer welcome – or safe – in this country."

"Then we must leave," said Val. "Right away." She looked around. The desert that had always fascinated her was quickly turning into a place to be feared.

"The young woman is right," Machmoud said quietly. The look on his face was as strong as his words. "You must leave as quickly as you can."

CHAPTER

4

Escape Plan

Inside Selk's tent, Machmoud was helping the archaeologist plan the best route for leaving Kalim. The two men sat at a table, a map of the country spread out before them. Bruce and Val looked over their shoulders. A small oil lamp threw a warm yellow light across the room.

"I believe we should head for Lantum," Selk began. He pointed on the map to a small country north of Kalim. "The government there was friendly with the old government here, and I think they would allow us in. We'll have to cross the Ur River that runs between the countries. But if we can do that, we'll be all right. What do you think, Machmoud?"

The Arab's headpiece threw a shadow onto his face. "It is the best way," he agreed. "But you must remember that any way you travel can be dangerous. The desert is a hard home. Even those who are used to it can lose their way. Besides worrying about the rebels, you may run out of water, come across robbers . . . ." Machmoud looked hard at Selk. "I hope you have not been away so long that you have forgotten the dangers."

Selk smiled in a strange way. "I have not forgotten," he said quietly.

As she listened to Selk's answer, Val suddenly saw in her mind a picture of the trip that faced them. She saw the wide, endless desert and the burning sun. She saw the party's jeep, a dark dot on the white sand. She could almost feel the heat and her dry throat asking for water. She could see robed people coming toward them. But she blinked her eyes and made the picture go away. If crossing the desert to Lantum was the best way out of the country, that was the way they would go.

But Bruce seemed troubled. "The heat," he said. "I don't know if I can take a long trip like that." He looked from Val to Selk. "And I can't believe the rebels would really hurt us."

Selk looked at Bruce with a face that showed little. "I won't force you to cross the desert, Bruce," he said. "But it seems the best thing to do. If we stay here or go back to the capital, we don't know what will happen. The rebels might put us on a plane out of the country – or they might do something much worse."

"All right, all right," said Bruce. "I'll go." He stared at the map, a worried look on his face. Val wondered if he was seeing the same picture of the desert that she had just seen.

Selk stood up. "It's settled then," he said. "We'll pack tonight and leave before the sun comes up. Machmoud," he said, taking his friend's hand. "Thank you for warning us. But now you should go too. It would not be good if it was known that you helped us."

Machmoud nodded, then bowed to the three of them. He turned quickly and walked out into the night.

Selk looked at Val and Bruce before following Machmoud out of the tent. "Pack only what you need," he said. "I will ask Ali to come with us and show the way to the river."

Walking fast, Selk left the tent and called to Ali. Quickly the dark-eyed man appeared, and Selk told him what had happened and what they planned to do. Ali listened, saying nothing. When Selk asked if he would take them to the river, Ali said only, "Of course."

As Selk went to take care of the statue, Ali gave the order to his workers to pack up the camp. Val could hear the men calling to each other and the sounds of the packing as she gathered her own things. Then she lay down and tossed and turned until sleep finally came. When Bruce called to her before dawn the next morning, she still felt worn out.

Val dressed quickly, putting on one of the long, white robes everyone would be wearing for the trip. When she stepped into the still-dark morning, she could see Selk, Ali, and Bruce loading one of the dig's two jeeps with food, water, and other supplies. The golden statue, with its strange smile, was already safely on board.

Val began to help with the loading as Selk moved off to thank the Arab workers. They were leaving to return to their homes in the other jeep. As sand flew in the jeep's wake, Selk walked back to his own jeep to check the supplies.

Finally all was ready. Selk got behind the steering wheel, with Ali beside him. Val and Bruce climbed into the back. The engine roared as the jeep dug its giant tyres into the sand and began moving forward.

Val turned for a last look at the dig as a ribbon of light broke through the deep purple sky. The piles of dirt and rock were still there, but no people stood around them. Now the place had a lonely look. Val watched it grow smaller and wondered if anything was still hidden there.

* * *

As the loaded jeep worked its way north, Val's thoughts were on the dangers they faced. But the hours went by, and another worry began to buzz in her head. In the excitement of the night before, she had forgotten about Selk's strange behaviour in the tunnel. Now she remembered. She wondered if the statue was the only important thing in the jeep. She would have to find out sooner or later if Selk had really stolen something for himself.

"Listen," Bruce said. His voice sounded tired but angry. "All the rebels will do is send us out of the country. They won't hurt us. Why not just turn ourselves in? Wouldn't it be easier?"

"Even if they didn't hurt us, what about the statue?" Val asked in an angry voice of her own. She looked at Selk's face, then at Bruce. "Do we just let them take it and melt it down for the gold?"

Bruce shook his head. Then he laughed. "Well, we can't drive back, we can't go to the oasis, and we can't stay here." He tried to laugh again, but what came out was a scared sound. "We'll just have to fly!" he finally shouted, hitting his leg and looking around. But no one found this very funny, and finally Bruce was quiet.

No one said anything until Ali spoke up. "There is a small oasis further north," he said. "It is still three hours away from here, but it should be safe."

CHAPTER

5

Night Watch

The hours passed slowly. When the sun went down, the desert air was cool, but the ride was still hard. Without the awful sun, Bruce felt much better, but like everyone else, he was just waiting for the second oasis.

Finally Ali said that the tree-ringed watering area was nearby. Once again he left the jeep. He walked quickly away from the low lights and into the darkness.

This time Ali returned much sooner. He spoke quietly to Selk and then directed the jeep forward. In a few moments, the shapes of rounded palm trees and a small, dark pool of water came into view. Selk parked the jeep near one of the smaller trees.

"I've never been so glad to be on my own two feet before," Val said. She felt sore all over.

Bruce lifted his arms over his head. "It still feels like I'm in that jeep," he said. "My body may never stop jumping. Let's walk around to the other side of the oasis to get the knots out."

"No." It was Ali who spoke. "We must make camp quickly so our lights will not be seen." Then he pointed to the far side of the water and a group of trees. "We share this oasis tonight. We must remain where we are."

Val looked surprised. "Who are we sharing it with?" She and Bruce stared into the dark.

"With some Bedouins – the desert people," Selk answered. He pointed toward a dark shape that looked like a large rock. Careful looking, however, showed that the shape was not a rock, but three Bedouins wrapped head to toe in dark blankets. "Ali has already spoken to them. They didn't want us to stay here, but he gave them money and promised that we wouldn't make trouble. Let's set up camp now."

As they worked, Bruce kept an eye on the quiet figures under the trees. They made no noise and seemed to be asleep. Suddenly Bruce saw something moving behind them. It was tall, with a rounded back. Of course, a camel, Bruce thought. Then another animal moved up next to the first. Light from the moon showed two more camels resting on the ground.

Once camp had been made and dinner eaten, Selk spoke quietly to the group. "Ali has told me that robbers often come to this oasis. For that reason, one of us will have to stay awake at all times. We can't leave the statue – or our supplies – without a guard. Bruce, I'd like you to take first watch. You seem to have got some sleep on the trip. In two hours, wake Val. Val, you wake me after two hours. And I will wake Ali to stand watch last."

Selk looked at Val and Bruce and smiled a tired smile. "I know how you feel," he said. "We've all had a long day. If you think you can't make it, Ali and I can take turns, and you can sleep."

Val shook her head. "I'll take my turn," she said. "Me too," Bruce quickly agreed. As everyone else lay down to rest, he started walking around the camp. The night was growing cooler, and he swung his arms to keep warm.

It seemed like no time at all to Val before Bruce was shaking her, telling her to get up. "Is everything OK? How did you keep from falling asleep?" she asked him. She sat up slowly, rubbing her eyes.

"I kept walking," he told her. "I walked around and around the jeep the whole time. I think I'm tired enough to die." He rolled his head and closed his eyes. "I keep wondering if our golden god is worth all the trouble."

Val snapped awake. "Of course, it is. It may turn out to be one of the most important finds ever made."

"Maybe," Bruce said in a low voice. "But I'm not sure how important it is to *me.*" He walked over to his blanket and lay down.

Shaking her head, Val stood up and headed for the jeep. As she walked, she saw one of the Bedouins standing by the camels. He must be standing guard too, she thought. He seemed to be looking at her as she stopped to splash water on her face. When she stood and continued toward the jeep, he still seemed to be looking at her. I guess he's never seen an American in a desert robe, she thought – not a woman anyway.

Looking in the back of the jeep, Val found the statue still wrapped in brown blankets and tied with rope. Patting it, she began to walk around the jeep. All was quiet as she looked up at the trees. But somewhere out there beyond the oasis, she knew, rebel police were looking for outsiders. And robbers might be close by too. It was still a long way to the Ur River.

Val stopped. She thought she had heard a soft noise. She listened for a moment, but the sound didn't come again. Nothing was moving. Just ghosts, she told herself with a small smile.

Then all at once, her head seemed to explode. Val saw stars. Everything went dark.

The next thing she knew, someone was shaking her and calling her name. She opened her eyes. Ali was bending over her, a ribbon of orange light breaking through the sky behind him.

"What?" said Val. "What . . . happened?" She tried to sit up, but her head hurt too much to move.

"They have taken the jeep," said Ali, his dark eyes staring back at Val.

"What?" Val said. "Who?"

"The Bedouins, I believe," Ali told her. "They are gone now. They must have hit you and then taken the jeep."

Val tried to sit up again, holding her head. "I feel awful," she said. Then the thought hit her. "The golden god!" she cried.

Ali nodded. "It is gone too, of course. It was in the jeep." And he walked off to get Selk.

Val felt as though she were caught in a terrible dream. The statue was gone and it quickly became clear to her that they were all alone now in the middle of the desert – with no way to travel on. What could they do? She could not make her hurting head think of a way out.

When Val saw Selk running toward her, she struggled to her feet. "Dr. Selk!" she called. "I'm so sorry!"

But Selk didn't answer. He just looked past her, to the spot where the jeep had been. It was as if he hoped that what Ali had told him wasn't true. When he saw that it was, he look at Val, his face red.

"How could you –?" he began, his voice full of anger. But he stopped when he saw the look on Val's face. Talking under his breath, he turned toward Ali.

Then Bruce ran up. "I heard Ali telling you," he shouted excitedly to Selk. "What will we do without the jeep? We can't *walk* across the desert. How will we get away?" He was breathing hard, his hair pressed to his head.

Ali answered with a calm look toward the palm trees beyond them. "They have left behind their camels," he said. "We will ride them."

Val looked. Sure enough, the camels were there. She let out a long breath.

Now Selk turned back toward Val. Again he looked past her, not at her, but this time his voice was more quiet. "You're not to blame for what happened. None of us knew we were sharing the oasis with thieves. Let's just get started. Maybe we can get the statue back."

Quickly everyone gathered the few belongings they could tie to their saddles – food, water, and blankets. Everything else would be left behind. While they did this, Ali saddled the camels and led them over to Val and the others. Up close, the animals looked mean and smelt bad. They swung their long necks around and drew back their lips over their long teeth.

Ali gave one of the camels near Val a tap on the neck. The big animal gave Ali a mean look. Then it sank slowly to its knees.

"This is the easiest way to load a camel," he told Val. "And the only way to get on."

Val tied on her supplies as Ali showed the others how to make their camels kneel and to secure their belongings. Then Val climbed on her camel. The camel struggled to its feet, jerking back and forth. She felt herself being lifted high above the ground.

Bruce and Selk mounted their camels as Ali watched. Then swinging easily onto the last camel, Ali waved the group out into the desert. They would follow the wheel tracks of the jeep back the way they had come from the first oasis.

The camels moved with a slow, rolling walk, lifting the riders up and down with each step. The jerking deepened the pain in Val's head, the pain that made it impossible to forget what had happened. She closed her eyes and saw the Bedouin watching her. Then she saw the golden statue's green eyes and its knowing smile.

Val opened her own eyes and watched Selk on the camel in front of her. He looked small. Then she remembered that afternoon at the dig. She remembered seeing Selk reach down and pick something up. She remembered the small bag disappearing into the pocket. And later there had been the strange look on his face when she asked if he had found anything.

She was still wondering if she would ever find out what had happened when Bruce rode past her. He moved his camel up next to Selk. "This is crazy," Val heard him say. "Why are we doing this? Chasing people in a jeep on camels. What chance could we have of catching up with them?"

"We have one chance, Bruce," said Selk. "The jeep was almost out of petrol when we stopped last night. The petrol can is stored under the floor in the back. It may take the Bedouins quite a while to find it. The jeep should have run out of petrol after two or three miles, we may still be able to catch up with them."

"And then what?" asked Bruce.

Selk's face was quiet. "We'll see," he answered.

Bruce stopped his camel and waited for Val as Selk moved ahead. When he was next to Val, he spoke quickly. "Dr. Selk should just face it – the statue is gone, and we won't get it back. I think it's better this way. Without it, we're not in so much danger. If the police find us, or if we turn ourselves in, all they would do is send us out of the country. And that's all I want – to get out of this place."

Val looked at him. Her mouth turned down as though she'd tasted something bad. "You sound like you're glad the statue was stolen," she said to Bruce. "What's happened to your love of ancient things? You're beginning to sound like all you care about is saving your own skin."

Bruce opened his mouth to answer. But before he could speak, Ali's voice cut in. "Look!" he called pointing at the ground ahead. The line of tyre tracks they had been following now crossed another set of tracks. A wide circle of sand had been pushed about.

"It looks as if they stopped here," said Selk, staring at the ground. "And met another jeep."

"Police," Ali said. "The other tracks come from the first oasis. It looks as if there was a fight." Ali nodded at a dark patch on the sand.

"Blood?" asked Selk.

"I think so," Ali said.

"Then the people who stole the statue are in the hands of the police now," Selk said slowly. And so was the golden god – Selk didn't have to say that. Everyone in the group knew that the statue was probably lost forever.

Selk's face had lost its colour. His eyes had gone blank. "We'd better start heading toward Lantum again," he said in a low, dull voice. "Nothing we can do here."

"Yes," said Ali. "Besides, we are only a few miles from the Rhani Oasis. The rebel police will be close by."

They turned around. Ali led the way, following the tracks their camels had made. Selk rode close behind Ali. Val, who followed, looked at her teacher's bent back and shook her head. Selk seemed suddenly like an old man. His dream of finding the ancient city in Kalim had just ended. Behind her, Bruce was probably just as unhappy, but for another reason.

No one talked as the camels walked along. The sun was burning down again, and the sky looked as hard and bright as steel. Val started to close her eyes.

Suddenly Ali stopped his camel and was lowered to the ground. He peered at the sand near his feet. "Here are some tracks I did not see before," he said, "Footsteps. It looks as if someone walked this way, then tried to wipe away the tracks." A broken line of prints could be seen leading off to the west.

"What do you think it means?" Selk asked, looking down.

Ali shrugged. "Let's follow and find out," he said. Then he peered around. "Where is Bruce?" he asked.

"Probably just over that hill," Val said, waving. "He was a little way behind me."

"All right," said Ali. "He'll see our tracks and follow."

The three of them moved off toward the west. Sometimes they saw no prints for several paces, but there was always another further ahead. They pushed on for about 10 minutes. Then Ali came to a stop.

"The tracks seem to end here," he said. He looked hard at the area. Then he got down from his camel and pointed. "Look over here, at this small bush. All around it, the wind has made lines on the sand. But here there are no lines. The sand has been smoothed by something or someone."

"No one would spread a blanket to rest in the middle of the desert," Selk said, thinking out loud. "And why would a traveller leave the path he was following, sit down here, and then go back to the path? It makes no sense."

Ali dropped to his knees in the sand. "Perhaps not," he said. "But what if the traveller was carrying something important? And what if he saw, coming toward him in the distance, someone he thought might want to take it away from him? He might run off quickly to hide it. And he might bury it in a place where he'd be able to find it again – such as next to this bush."

As he was talking, Ali began digging in the sand. In a moment, he had uncovered something brown. Quickly Val and Selk brought their camels to the ground and jumped down.

As they dug along with Ali, the hole he had started grew bigger.

"It's the statue," Val whispered as the rope-tied object came into view.

"It's the statue!" she said again, shouting this time. She watched excitedly as Ali undid the ropes and the smiling face appeared.

"Ali!" said Selk. "You've found it!" He jumped to his feet. His face had come to life again. "I cannot thank you enough."

Ali just smiled. "It is good," he said. "But we should take the statue and leave right away."

Val couldn't stop smiling as she helped Ali and Selk load the heavy statue onto the side of one of the camels, and move a heavy load of supplies onto the other side. The return of the green-eyed god would make all the worry and the trouble of the trip easier to bear. Everyone seemed much happier until Selk suddenly looked around. "Where's Bruce?" he asked.

Val's mouth dropped open in surprise. In the excitement of finding the statue, she had not even thought about Bruce. He certainly should have caught up with them by now. But he wasn't in sight.

CHAPTER

6

The Endless Desert

"Where could he be?" asked Selk. Like Val, he couldn't believe Bruce hadn't caught up with them yet.

But Val began to nod her head. "I think I know," she said quietly. "He could have followed our tracks if he had wanted to. But this whole trip has been hard for him. He's been sure the rebel police would be easier to take than the long, hot days in the desert. I think he wanted out. I think he's headed back to the Rhani Oasis to turn himself in."

Ali closed his eyes and shook his head. "He's a fool," he said.

"You don't think they'll kill him, do you?" Val put her hand on Ali's arm.

Ali didn't speak.

"I don't know," Selk answered instead. "But they'll wonder where he came from."

"Bruce wouldn't tell them about us, though," Val said quickly. "He may not be happy with the way things turned out, but he wouldn't do anything like that."

Selk just looked at her. "I'm sure he doesn't *plan* to tell them anything. But people who have just come to power are often very good at making others say more than they want to."

"What has he done?" Val said in a low voice. She looked at the ground.

"He has made his decision," Selk answered, his voice once again calm. "There is nothing we can do about it. Going after him would just put four people in danger instead of one." He looked at the statue tied to the camel's saddle. "I'm sorry about Bruce – very sorry. But we must go on."

"And quickly," Ali added. "If the police learn anything from Bruce, they will come looking for us."

With one last look around, the small group climbed onto the camels and set out again for Lantum. Val couldn't help thinking about Bruce. What would happen to him at the oasis? Why had he been so stupid? Half of Val was worried about Bruce, and the other half was angry with him. She wondered if she could have said anything that would have made him see how foolish it was to go back.

Time passed slowly as the sun once again made the air almost too hot to breathe. Each hill of sand looked like the one before it and gave off waves of heat. Though the trip seemed days long, the sun stayed high in the sky. Val wondered if evening would ever come. Her head swimming, she called out to Ali, "Is there any water left?"

"A little," said Ali, stopping his camel. He passed her a canteen. "Drink only a small amount," he told her. "The water must last us until tonight."

Val put the canteen to her lips. The water was warm and unpleasant. It didn't help much. She began to feel weak, but she moved her camel forward again.

The drink of water had helped Val's dry throat, but it hadn't helped her tired body come back to life. She began to think she must be more than just tired. The sand was starting to look red, and a ringing began in her head.

Val shook herself weakly. "I can make it," she kept saying in a whisper. "All I have to do is hang on."

But after a while, the words stopped meaning anything. They were just sounds, just a buzzing like the heat that seemed to close in around her. Finally darkness swam in front of her eyes. She tried to call out, but she couldn't tell if any words came from her mouth. Leaning back, she closed her eyes, and the darkness took over.

The next thing Val knew, she was flat on her back and looking up into Ali's lined face. For a second, she couldn't remember what had happened. Then her mind cleared. "I passed out, didn't I?" she said. Her voice came out cracked and dry.

Selk's face came into view above her. "You did. And you're going to need some rest now," he said. He looked worried.

"But there's no time," Val said. She started to sit up. "I'll be all right." But as she spoke, another wave of black rose up before her eyes. She lay down again, her head pounding.

"You need some rest," Selk said again. His long fingers brushed the hair away from her face. "We'll make camp and spend the night here. The police probably won't be on our trail until morning."

There was nothing Val could say. She drank the water Ali brought her. Then she lay still, her eyes closed, while he and Selk set up camp. She knew that stopping now was putting the group in great danger. She told herself that getting sick from the heat wasn't her fault – but it didn't really help. As she fell off to sleep, she began to feel more kindly toward Bruce and what he had been going through all summer.

It was dark when Val awoke just before morning, and the air was cool. Her head was clear, her body rested. She felt better. But she knew that even if she hadn't felt well, she would have made herself go on anyway. Quickly she rolled up her sleeping bag and had a drink from the canteen.

"How do you feel today?" Selk asked as she walked toward her camel. He was standing next to his own camel, making sure that the statue was still safely tied on.

"Much better thanks," Val answered. "I don't think I'll fall off again, anyway." She pulled some dried fruit from her pack and tied on her sleeping bag.

"Time to get started," Ali called. He was already on his camel waiting for the other two. "The sun will be up soon."

Val tapped her camel's neck to kneel. Then she swung herself on and held tightly to the saddle while the heavy animal got to its feet. From the camel's back, Val looked around. The sky was black overhead. But off in the east, the direction they had come from, a bright place showed where the sun would soon come up. As the camels began to move, Val kept looking at this bright spot. There was something strange about it. It seemed to be moving – but not the way the sun would move.

"Look!" she called to Selk and Ali, pointing. The two men turned around. "What is –" she began. But then Val heard a low roar, and she understood what she had been seeing. Headlights. And they were getting closer by the second.

CHAPTER

7

Danger at Dawn

"Get down from your camels," Ali said quietly. "Lie by them on the ground, and do not move."

Val and Selk did as he said. Lying very still, hardly breathing, Val listened to the roar of the motor. It was getting louder. And every moment the sky was growing lighter. Soon the three camels and the people beside them would show clearly against the desert sand. Val didn't think there was much hope they would be missed.

She was right. Before long the sound of the motor filled her ears. She could see, even without lifting her head, the cloud of dust kicked up by spinning wheels.

"They've caught us," Val said. There was no

need to keep quiet any longer.

"As God wills," said Ali, his voice empty. He stood up. Val and Selk stood up too. The headlights of a truck were shining right on them. When it was only yards away, it jerked to a stop, and two soldiers jumped out. Both of them held guns. One shouted something in Arabic, and Selk and Ali raised their hands above their heads. Seeing them, Val did the same.

The tall soldier who had shouted walked up to Selk. The other one kept his gun pointed at the group. The tall soldier spoke quickly to Selk in a high, angry voice. He seemed to be asking questions. Selk answered, his voice calm and low. Whatever the answer was, it did not please the soldier. He shouted something at Selk. Then he shouted an order to the other soldier.

The second soldier walked around to the back of the truck and opened its doors. Val heard yelling and then a bumping noise. Finally the soldier appeared again, pulling another person by the arm. Val took in a sharp breath. The other person was Bruce.

He looked terrible. His face was dirty, his clothes a mess. It looked like the skin around one eye was turning black. Heavy-looking handcuffs locked his hands together in front of him.

The tall soldier started to talk to Selk again. Val could not understand what he was saying though. And she threw Ali a questioning look.

"He says he knows we have something with us that belongs to his people," Ali said. "They found the photo of the statue in Bruce's things . . . ."

The tall soldier shouted something, and Ali stopped talking. Val was left again to guess at what was being said.

The soldier seemed to bark an order at Selk. His face set in hard lines, Selk walked toward the camel that carried the golden god. He began to unpack the statue.

Val looked at Ali. The man's face was blank. She looked at Bruce. The second soldier still held his arm, but Bruce was looking straight at her. Then he moved his mouth without making a sound. He was trying to tell her something. But she couldn't make out what it was.

She made a puzzled face to let Bruce know that she didn't understand. She couldn't do more, in case the soldiers saw her making a sign. What was Bruce saying? She tried hard to figure out the words he had said.

Val looked back at Selk. He had the statue on the ground now and was starting to unwrap it. Both soldiers moved forward to see. They pushed Val, Ali, and Bruce along with the points of their guns.

Again Val looked at Bruce. Again he tried to tell her something. First he looked down at the heavy handcuffs he wore. Then he looked at the head of the shorter soldier. Finally he looked at the tall soldier and made three words with his mouth. It looked like *Et the ud . . .* or *Et the gud . . .* No! *Get the gun!* All at once Val knew what Bruce was trying to tell her. He would hit the shorter soldier over the head, and she was to get the gun from the other one.

Val tried not to show the surprise and excitement she felt. It was a crazy plan, a dangerous one. But there was a chance it might work. As calmly as she could, she made a quick nod at Bruce to show she understood.

Selk was pulling away the last blanket from the statue. In seconds the golden god lay flashing in the first light of the sun. The two soldiers stared, their mouths open, forgetting everything but the sight that filled their eyes. For a moment, they even forgot to hold tightly to their guns. That moment was all it took.

Bruce raised his handcuffed hands and brought them down hard on the shorter soldier's head. The man groaned as he dropped to the ground, and the tall soldier spun around to see what was happening. As he turned, Val reached out and grabbed his gun. Quickly he caught at her arm, trying to get hold of it. And then there was a terrible bang.

Somehow the bullet missed everyone.

Then Ali came to life. Seeing what was happening, he threw himself at the tall soldier. The man went down, and Val kept hold of the gun. Then Bruce hit the other soldier again, and Selk grabbed his gun.

"Ali!" cried Selk. "Here, take this rope. Tie these two up." He kicked over to Ali the rope that had held the golden god, keeping the gun pointed at the soldiers.

"What are we going to do with them?" Val asked, watching Ali tie the last knot.

"We'll leave them here with the camels," said Selk. "They will get free. But it will take time — enough time for us to cross the river."

"Let us hurry," Ali said. He began to help Selk move their things from the camels into the truck.

While the two men worked, Val set about getting Bruce free from his handcuffs. She found a key-ring on one of the soldiers, then tried a few of the keys until the heavy locks snapped apart. The soldier stared hard at Val and spoke some sharp, angry words. But she just smiled back at him.

Soon the golden god was packed safely into the back of the truck, and everyone climbed in. The engine coughed, then roared loudly, and the truck moved off across the sand with its passengers.

Selk pushed open the window between the front seat and the back. Val and Bruce were riding there with the statue. "I want to thank you both for what you did back there. It saved the statue — and us."

"It was Bruce's idea," Val told him.

"It was the only smart thinking I've done for a long time," Bruce said in a low voice. "I guess I've been a fool. All I wanted back there was to get you out of the danger I had put you in."

"You mean you told those guys where we'd gone?" Val asked him sharply.

"I didn't have to tell them," answered Bruce. "When I showed up at the oasis, they found out who I was. They knew you had to be nearby." He shook his head sadly. "I was so wrong about them," he said.

"What made you go to them, Bruce?" Selk asked.

Bruce leaned back. "I just couldn't face going across the desert any more. It was making me crazy, all the heat and running. I thought we would die in this terrible place. I knew I couldn't make the rest of you change your minds. So I decided to go off by myself.

"When I got to the oasis," Bruce went on, "The soldiers grabbed me right away. They took me to an officer who spoke a little English. He asked me questions. Where was I from? What was I doing here? Who had I been with? I told him I was an American, and I just wanted to leave his country. He laughed.

"They searched my things and found my

papers. As soon as they knew I'd been part of the dig, they wanted to know what we had found. I told them there was nothing, but they didn't believe me."

Bruce closed his eyes as if remembering everything had made him tired. "Then they found the photo of the golden god," he said. "After that, they beat me. I didn't tell them anything. But they knew you were out here somewhere. The truck set out to look for you early this morning."

"How many rebels were at the oasis?" asked Selk.

"Not many," Bruce told him. "I saw only five or six. That's why they sent out only two in the truck — they didn't have enough men for a bigger search."

"Good," said Selk. "They won't miss these two for some time. And they're not likely to send anyone else out looking for us. We should be safe for several hours." He sat back in his seat and looked out across the bright desert.

"How long before we get to the river, Ali?" asked Val.

Ali's eyes found her in the mirror. "Now that we have this truck," he said, "by evening — if everything goes well."

CHAPTER

8

The River at Last

Hour after hour went by. Sometimes Val turned around and looked out of the back of the truck. She was searching the desert for dark dots that could be rebel jeeps or trucks coming after them. But she saw only sand and sky. Bruce lay beside her, tossing as he slept.

Val tried to rest, keeping her mind blank and free of fears or worries. But there were a few thoughts she couldn't keep out — thoughts about Selk. Again the picture came to her of Selk picking up something at the dig, putting it in a clear bag, and hiding the bag in his pocket. She would have to find out why he had done that. Or she might never be able to work with him again. But she would wait until they had crossed the river and all the danger was behind them.

At last the sun began to sink in the west. "The river should not be far away now," said Ali from the front of the truck. "At the river there is a bridge, and on this side of it a crossing station. We will stay away from there, since rebel police will surely have taken it over. We will try to cross about a mile further up, where there's a small town. There are sure to be some boats nearby. Keep your eyes open now for signs of the station or the town."

But for a long time, there was no sign of anything at all. The sky turned a dark blue, and the stars came out. Bruce finally woke up and looked around.

"No moon tonight," said Ali. "That's good — the darkness will help to hide us."

They bumped along through the night. Knowing that they would have fresh supplies soon, they ate what was left of their food. Val was passing the canteen through the window to Selk when suddenly she saw light in the distance.

"Look!" she said. "A light! Do you think it's the town?"

"We'll have to get closer before we can tell," said Ali.

They rode on in silence. In a few minutes, Ali spoke again quietly. "It's the town. See how the lights are low and spread out? The crossing station would shine just one light, very bright."

Everyone breathed deeply as Ali guided the truck south of the town, away from houses and roads. Finally the fast-moving river came into view. It shone like a wide ribbon of silver.

They pulled up next to it and climbed quickly out of the truck. Ali began searching for a boat along the bank. Bruce watched Ali as he moved farther and farther up the river. Soon Ali disappeared into the darkness.

"Do you think he's in trouble?" Bruce asked several minutes later when Ali still hadn't returned.

"No, he's all right," Selk whispered. "Look!" He pointed up the river.

Ali was in a small boat, coming toward them. In a minute or so, he nosed the boat toward the shore. Then he jumped out where the water was less deep and pulled the boat after him. "It's very small," he said, looking down at it. "But there was no time to look for another. Get in quickly."

"First the statue," said Selk. He and Bruce unloaded the heavy object from the truck. With Ali's help, they put it in the boat. Right away the boat settled a little lower into the water. Ali pulled it into a deeper part of the river. Then he pointed to Bruce, who was closest to him. "You get in first."

Bruce splashed out to the boat and climbed in. The weighted boat rocked back and forth and went lower still. Then Val got in. The boat dropped again, leaving only about twenty centimetres above the water.

"This is bad," Ali said. "The boat will float holding one more person, but not two. Someone will have to stay behind. We'll have to make two trips."

"I'll stay," said Selk. "You go ahead," he told Ali. "Get the statue and yourselves across first. Then one of you can come back for me." He waved them off and sat down on the bank to wait.

Ali got into the boat and used an oar to push away from shore. Then he locked the oars in place and began to row.

No one spoke. The only sounds were the rushing of the river and the groaning of the oars. Val kept her eyes fixed on the far shore. Little by little, it came closer. But as it did, the water began to move faster. Ali had to row hard to keep the boat moving across the current.

"Val," he said, "come and take an oar. Bruce, keep the statue from hitting the sides."

Val changed seats, moving carefully to keep from upsetting the boat. But when she sat down beside Ali, the boat tipped to one side, letting water pour in. Now the top of the boat was barely out of the water.

"Pull hard!" cried Ali, water splashing around his feet. Val pulled with all her might, but as smoothly as she could. She knew that if any more water came over the side, the boat would sink.

The roar of the racing water filled their ears as they struggled. The old boards of the boat seemed to be crying out against this hard use. But at last the bank they had left looked very far away.

"We're almost there," Bruce called. "Just a little farther."

Then all at once, there was a loud crack. Ali fell backward, and his oar seemed to jump out of his hand. The boat swung sideways, rocking wildly, and water poured in over the side.

"The oarlock broke!" cried Bruce. "Grab the oar!"

But it was too late. When Ali had fallen backward, he had lost his hold on the oar. Before he could grab it again, it had slipped over the side of the boat and floated away.

Bruce yelled to Val. "See if you can use your oar to paddle on both sides." Already the fast-moving current had caught them and was pulling them down, instead of across, the river.

"We'll have to get out," Ali said. "Or we'll be carried right down to the crossing station. It doesn't look too deep here. I'll test it."

"What about the statue?" Val asked as Ali started to move.

"We'll hang onto the boat when we're out," he told her. "Maybe we can pull it to shore with us." He lowered himself into the water, which stopped at his chest. At his nod, Bruce and Val climbed over the side. Pulling the heavy boat, they struggled toward the shore.

The water pushed them sideways. Several times they lost their footing and almost fell. But no one let go of the boat. As they hung on, the water finally sank to their hips, then to their knees. With one last, tired pull, they dragged the boat out of the current and fell to the ground. They were safe — and so was the golden god. But Selk was alone on the other side of the river, and the boat couldn't make it back there.

CHAPTER

9

Waiting for Selk

After a few minutes, Val got to her feet and looked across the river. It was too dark to see the other side. But she wondered if Selk could have seen what happened to them in the middle of the river.

"We can't help Dr. Selk," Ali said. "His safety, I am afraid, is now up to him."

"But the rebels . . .," Val began. Then she stopped. She knew Ali was right.

"We must walk down to the bridge," Ali went on. "It should not be far — less than a mile, I think. There is a station also on this side — the Lantum side. Maybe someone there could get help to Dr. Selk. If not, then I will look for him when I return to Kalim."

They set out into the darkness, their wet

clothes sticking to their skin. The heavy gold statue made them walk slowly, and the short distance seemed to take forever to cover.

Finally they saw a light. As they got closer, they saw that it came from a small building that stood next to a long, flat bridge.

"The station," said Ali. "Let's hope they welcome us."

When they reached the building, Ali told Bruce and Val to stay outside with the statue. "I'll go in alone," he told them. "If you hear trouble, hide."

Quietly he went to the door of the building and walked inside. The door closed behind him. Bruce and Val could hear the sound of two or three voices speaking in Arabic.

Suddenly the door opened again. Ali came out, followed by two soldiers. The soldiers came up to Val and Bruce and peered at them closely. Finally one of the men said something and pointed toward the building. "He is telling us to come in," Ali said to Bruce and Val. He helped them lift the heavy statue and take it inside.

It was a small room with a desk, table and several chairs. Bruce dropped onto one chair, and Val sank down thankfully onto another.

She looked at the wrapped statue at her feet. She remembered the discovery of the small stone room — the start of their adventure. She wondered if the adventure was ever going to end.

For a long time, Ali talked to the soldiers. Often they shook their heads sadly and shrugged their shoulders. At last Ali turned to Val and Bruce. "They say they can do nothing to help Dr. Selk," he said. "Lantum and Kalim are not friendly right now. People from one country are not welcome in the other. All we can do, at least until the morning, is wait."

One of the soldiers had sent for some dry robes for the three visitors. He also brought them coffee, bread, and dates to quiet their empty stomachs. Warm and full, Ali and Bruce soon fell asleep. But Val stayed wide awake.

She thought about Selk, alone on the far side of the river. She wondered if he would think of a way to get out of the country safely. Or would he be caught and beaten and handcuffed like Bruce. Maybe he was already in the hands of the rebels. Maybe he would never be heard from again.

At last the blackness outside the windows of the station began to change to grey. Val went outside and watched the sun come up far out over the desert they had crossed. The sky became a bright pink. The sand in the distance looked calm and beautiful. How different it all looks from this side of the river, Val thought.

All at once she saw something moving on the bridge. It was a jeep coming from the other side. She watched with growing fear. Rebel soldiers? She hurried into the station.

"A jeep is coming across the bridge," she told the others. Ali and the two soldiers stood up. One of the soldiers shook his head at Ali and then left the room.

"He wants us to stay here," Ali said. "In case there's trouble."

Val went to the window where she could see what was happening. The jeep came to a stop in front of the building, and an Arab in a white robe and red-checked headpiece got out. The driver, a man in a khaki shirt, said a few words to the soldier, then turned the jeep around and drove back across the bridge. The Arab came toward the station.

Val turned away from the window with a long breath. The jeep and the people in it had nothing to do with her. She felt let down and very tired.

Then the door opened, and the Arab came into the room. Val looked up, and her mouth opened in surprise. The Arab was Dr. Selk.

Bruce and Ali were on their feet now, too, crowding around Selk and asking him questions. Selk smiled. "Sit down," he said. "Sit down and I'll tell you what happened."

They pulled up their chairs. One of the soldiers made more coffee and passed cups to everyone. The morning light poured through the windows as Selk began talking.

"After you left in the boat," he said, "I watched you as long as I could. Though it was dark, I could see that you had trouble of some kind in the middle of the river. Then you got too far away for me to see what was happening. I waited a long time — maybe an hour. When you didn't come back, I knew something must have gone wrong.

Bruce explained how the oar had been lost, and Selk nodded. "I thought something like that had happened. That boat looked pretty sad and old."

Val smiled. "I think we carried it further than it carried us."

Selk nodded again, then went on with his story. "After a while, an idea came to me," he said. "I thought back to something that had happened at the dig. You remember that after we'd found the statue, we searched the area to see if anything else was hidden there. We found nothing — and that was very strange. Other things should have been there if my idea about the ancient city was right."

Selk set his coffee cup down and leaned back in his chair. "One afternoon," he went on, "I did find *something.* It was not of interest to our search, so I said nothing about it at the time." He shook his head. "But it turned out to be of very great worth."

Val almost dropped her cup. She looked sharply at Selk and then spoke. "What did you find?" she asked.

CHAPTER

10

The Secret

Selk seemed surprised by the hard look on Val's face. "I found a place where oil was coming up through the sand," he explained. "Often that's a sign of a pool of oil deep in the ground. Now, to some people, finding oil would have been an exciting discovery. To me, it meant only trouble. If anyone knew there was oil in that part of the desert, work at the dig would have been impossible. So I decided not to say anything about it. But I picked up a little of the oil-dotted sand and put it in a bag. I thought that after we had explored all we wanted in that spot, I'd let the oil people take a look at it."

"But you've already shown it to someone, haven't you?" Val asked.

Selk nodded. "I decided it was more help to me now than later. You see, after we found nothing else buried near the statue, I began to think I had been wrong about the ancient city. Not wrong to think there was a city — I still believe there was. Just wrong about where to find it. If it had been anywhere near our dig, we would have found *something* — before or after we found the statue."

"But the statue —," said Bruce.

"I know," said Selk. "I thought a lot about the statue. How could it have got there? At last I decided that it must have been *hidden* there, far away from the city. What if the people of the city had been at war? Maybe they had wanted to hide their most important thing in a place their enemies could not find.

"It seemed to me that's what they must have done . . . . As we rode across the desert, I thought about this a lot. It made more and more sense. And that meant that there was no reason to continue the dig at that spot."

"But you didn't tell us anything about that idea," said Val.

"It didn't seem the right time," said Selk. "After all, we were running for our lives. I felt that my thoughts on ancient cities could wait."

Bruce looked up from his black coffee. "I still don't understand," he said. "What does all this have to do with your getting across the river?"

"I'll tell you," Selk said. "As I sat there on the bank, wondering how to get across, I suddenly remembered that small bag of sand. It was still in my pocket, where I'd put it before we left. I took it out and looked at it. And an idea came to me. I knew just what I was going to do.

"First, I got rid of anything that would show who I am — my papers, my American shoes, everything. I made sure I looked as much like someone from Kalim as possible. And since I am a native, that was not too difficult. Then I started walking toward the crossing station. I knew the soldiers there might have heard about our escape from the other soldiers yesterday. They might be looking for me. But they'd be looking for an American archaeologist, not an ordinary-looking Arab. I thought I might have a chance to get past them."

"But the soldiers here tell me the rebels have not been allowing people to leave the country," said Ali. "Not even *ordinary* people. Why did you think they would let you?"

"That's where my little bag of sand came in," Selk said, smiling. "When I got to the station, I asked to speak to the head man. I tried to act like someone with little schooling who didn't know much about the world. I told the head man I needed to cross the river to see a friend in Lantum who was very ill. I told him I could pay him well to let me go.

"The head man laughed at this. I must not have looked as though I had anything he could possibly want. But when I brought out my little bag, he stopped laughing. 'Where did you get this?' he asked me. I said I would tell him if he would let me cross the river."

Selk shrugged. "Of course, he could have listened to what I said, then taken the sand and thrown me in jail. But I didn't think he would. It couldn't matter to him if I went across the river. In fact, letting me go would be less trouble for him than keeping me around."

"So you told him it came from the dig?" Val asked.

"Not in so many words," said Selk. "I drew a circle on the map." Selk drew a circle with his finger in the air and smiled at Val. It was a smile much like the one she had first seen long ago. "I could see he was in a hurry for me to leave. He wanted to rush off and tell people about the oil. He knew he would be cheered for having found it for the rebel government. So he called a jeep and had me driven across. And here I am."

Bruce shook his head. "What a story!"

"Indeed," Ali said, a smile spreading across his face. "You did well."

"And now everything is all right," Val said. She put down her coffee cup on the table beside her.

Selk put down his cup, too, and got up from his chair. In quick steps, he crossed the room to where the golden god lay, wrapped in its blankets. "Let's take a look at our friend," he said. "We've been through a lot with this old character." He took off the wrappings and stood the statue up against the wall. The morning sun flashed off the gold.

"Do you think it's really been our friend?" asked Bruce. "Maybe it's what brought us all that trouble. Maybe it does carry a curse."

"Maybe," said Val. "But think of all the lucky escapes we've had. If it had been bringing us bad luck, would things have turned out so well?"

She looked at Ali. He just smiled a strange smile.

"Well, would they?" Val asked again, louder.

Selk laughed then, and even Ali's smile broke into laughter.

"No, Val," Selk said. "We have been lucky in our adventures with the ancient statue." He patted the golden god on the head. "Now that Kalim is in rebel hands, we have only one last adventure to go through together. We have to get the statue to a museum in a free country."

One last adventure, Val thought. She joined the other archaeologists for a final cup of coffee before they said goodbye to Ali and set off on their way. In the corner, the golden god sat alone, a knowing smile on its face.